Little Wildflower

story by Jena Massie

illustrated by Jaylee Poindexter

WestBow Press books may be ordered through booksellers or by contacting:

WestBow Press
A Division of Thomas Nelson & Zondervan
1663 Liberty Drive
Bloomington, IN 47403
www.westbowpress.com
844-714-3454

Interior Image Credit: Jaylee Poindexter

ISBN: 978-1-6642-3836-7 (sc)
ISBN: 978-1-6642-3838-1 (hc)
ISBN: 978-1-6642-3837-4 (e)

Library of Congress Control Number: 2021912732

Print information available on the last page.

WestBow Press rev. date: 8/3/2021

WESTBOW
PRESS®
A DIVISION OF THOMAS NELSON
& ZONDERVAN

Little Wildflower

To my Saving Grace and Rescuer. The Bringer of butterflies
to dance my way, Grower of wildflowers through the broken
cracks, and One who gives the mockingbirds their melody.
You have stitched Eternity into my heart and my hope clings to you.

To my Mom, who has been the first editor of anything
I've ever written my whole entire life.

To Gracelyn and Alise, my first little wildflowers, whose giggles,
daydreams, and care-free spirits hold my heart together.

To my husband, Shawn, the protector of our light-heartedness, leader of
all our adventures and whose arms we wrap around every single day.
You are the heartbeat of our family.

To Sayge. You have irrevocably changed us all. We
will never forget what your love felt like.
You will always be my little wildflower on the other side of the stars.

And, to every girl who has ever dared to go on an adventure.
You light up this world.
Keep your heart wild and free.

The sun is waking up the day,
the little birds are singing.

The dew is shining across the grass, like glitter that is twinkling. The butterflies are dancing around the flowers in the sun...

Rise and shine, little wildflower,
adventure calls for fun!

There's so much to learn, so
much to go and see...

Get one last hug from Daddy's knee,
a goodbye kiss from mother.

Run out the door, and
out the gate, and out
to all the wonder.

A wishing flower waits for you,
to whisper what you dare,

all your hopes and
dreams, and silly
things, like flowers
in your hair!

Then 1, 2, 3, and a great big
wish, to watch its magic fly

across the breeze, and through the trees, like fairies dancing by!

Sunshine wants to kiss your hair.
Mud wants to paint your face.

Ladybugs want to sit on your shoulder.

Rainbows want to race.

Trees are waiting to be climbed.
"Let's see how high you can go!"

Butterflies want to tickle your fingers,
and land upon your nose...

To take a look, a closer one. At the
girl with freckles on her face.

Freckles sprinkled like the stars,
and is brand new to this place.

The girl whose spirit is carefree, has
Kind eyes filled with grace.

Who smells like flowers by the sea,
and always wants to race!

The girl who braids the Forget-Me-Nots

as a crown upon her hair,

daydreams about Forever, and
loves the animals with care.

As the day begins to slow, and the fireflies start their glowing, the sunshine splashes across the sky, and the day surrenders Knowing,

with a finger-painted masterpiece,
a pink and purple and blue blur,
one thing is for certain, it's been
a Heavenly one for her.

The little girl, with flowers in her hair,
has found her way back Home.

She's worth more than all the tomorrows,
and loved more than she'll ever know.

Our little wildflower, smiling and shining,
living life with every bit of her heart.

She has forever changed us all, with
all her wonder and spark.

Whether her adventures
keep her nearby, or puts
between us all the stars,

she leaves people better than when she found
them. Our wildflower. Our life. Our heart.

Printed in the United States
by Baker & Taylor Publisher Services